Lost! One bag

Characters

 Jamila Patel   Mr Miller

 Mrs Nash   Mr Crisp

 Mr Patel

Scenes

Scene 1   In Jamila's shop
Scene 2   In the shops
Scene 3   At Mrs Nash's house

Scene 1: In Jamila's shop

Jamila is helping her Dad in the shop. Mrs Nash comes in with her shopping bag.

Mr Patel: Hello, Mrs Nash.

Jamila: What can I get for you?

Mrs Nash: Quite a lot, Jamila.
(looking at her list)
I want to buy some bananas, some apples, a cake, some chicken and some of those lovely flowers.

Jamila: You get the flowers you want and I will get the other shopping.

 Mrs Nash: I think I will have some of those yellow flowers.
(She takes a bunch and puts them on the counter.)

 Jamila: (busy putting the rest of Mrs Nash's shopping on the counter)
Can you manage all this?
It will be quite heavy.

 Mrs Nash: Yes, I've not far to go.
I will manage the bag.

 Jamila: If you give me your bag, I will put the shopping in it for you.

 Mrs Nash: (getting her purse and handing the bag to Jamila)
Here you are, and here is some money.

 Jamila: Have you much shopping still to do?

 Mrs Nash: (taking the bag)
Not much, then I will go home and have some tea.
See you later.

(Mrs Nash leaves the shop.)

(Some time has passed.
Jamila is tidying the shelves when
Mrs Nash comes into the shop.)

Mr Patel: Hello again, Mrs Nash.
Did you forget something?

Mrs Nash: (Mrs Nash seems upset.)
Did I leave my bag here?
I can't find it.

Jamila: No, Mrs Nash.
When you left, you had it with you.

Mrs Nash: I didn't have it when I got home!

 Jamila: Where did you go when you left here?

 Mrs Nash: I went to the joke shop.

 Mr Patel: (sounding surprised)
The joke shop?

 Mrs Nash: Yes. I wanted to play a joke on Tony and Tessa after they gave me a fright with those masks.

 Jamila: Then where did you go?

 Mrs Nash: I went to Mr Crisp's fish and chip shop and then I went home.
I took my coat off and went to get my fish and chips, but I could not find my bag.

 Jamila: You go home, Mrs Nash.
I will go and look for your bag.

 Mr Patel: I'm sure Jamila will find your bag.

Scene 2: In the shops

Jamila is in Mr Miller's joke shop. Mr Miller is behind the counter.

Mr Miller: Hello, Jamila.
What can I do for you?

Jamila: I don't want to buy a joke, Mr Miller.
Mrs Nash can't find her bag.
Did she leave it here?

Mr Miller: (looking around)
I don't think she did.

Jamila: Can I look around?

Mr Miller: Yes, Jamila.
I will help you to look.

(Mr Miller and Jamila search around the shop.)

Jamila: I can't see it.

Mr Miller: No, it's not here, Jamila.

Jamila: I will try at the fish and chip shop.
(Jamila leaves the shop.)

(Jamila goes into the fish and chip shop. Mr Crisp is behind the counter.)

 Mr Crisp: Hello, Jamila.
What can I do for you?

Jamila: I don't want to buy fish and chips, Mr Crisp.
Mrs Nash can't find her bag.
Did she leave it here?

 Mr Crisp: I don't think so.

Jamila: Can I look around?

Mr Crisp: Yes, Jamila.
I will help you.

(Mr Crisp and Jamila look around the shop.)

Jamila: I can't see it.

Mr Crisp: No, it's not here, Jamila.
Where did Mrs Nash go when she left here?

Jamila: She went home.
She was going to have her fish and chips but she couldn't find her bag.

Mr Crisp: You will have to go and tell her that you couldn't find it.

Jamila: (looking worried)
Yes, I will.
She will be unhappy about it, but I will have to tell her.

Mr Crisp: I will ask people when they come into the shop if they have seen her bag.
Let me know if you find it.

Jamila: Yes I will, Mr Crisp.
I will come back and tell you if I find the bag.

(Jamila leaves the shop.)

Scene 3: At Mrs Nash's house

Jamila is in Mrs Nash's kitchen. Mrs Nash is sitting down looking upset.

Mrs Nash: Did you manage to find my bag, Jamila?
Did you manage to find it?

Jamila: (putting her hand on Mrs Nash's shoulder)
No, Mrs Nash.
I'm afraid I didn't manage to find it.

Mrs Nash: Where did you look?
Did you go to the joke shop?

Jamila: Yes. I went to see Mr Miller in the joke shop.
We looked around but we couldn't find it.

Mrs Nash: Where did you go next?

Jamila: I went to the fish and chip shop.

 Mrs Nash: (putting her head in her hands) And it wasn't there!

 Jamila: No, Mrs Nash.
Mr Crisp and I looked around but we couldn't find it.

 Mrs Nash: My fish and chips will be cold and all my money is gone!

 Jamila: (getting up and putting her arm around Mrs Nash)
Let's think what you did when you came home.
Did you put your bag down inside?

 Mrs Nash: No, I'm sure I didn't.
I took off my coat and I made some tea.
I don't know where I put my bag.

(There is a knock at the door.)

Jamila: I will see who that is.
(Jamila goes to the door and opens it.)
Hello, Mr Crisp.
We have not found the bag.

Mr Crisp: (holding up the bag)
But I have!

Mrs Nash: (coming to the door)
Oh, you have found my bag.
Where was it?

Mr Crisp: You must have gone through the park.
I found it on a bench.

Mrs Nash: Oh, yes! I did go through the park and sit on a bench.

Mr Crisp: Your fish and chips are cold but you have got your bag back!

(Everyone looks very pleased.)